THE KING OF AFFIRMATIONS SERIES PRESENTS:

THE KING OF

AFFIRMATIONS

PART 1
"RISE"

Michael "The Messiah" Ketter

PAGE PUBLISHING
Conneaut Lake, PA

First originally published by Page Publishing 2024

ISBN 979-8-89157-239-3 (pbk)
ISBN 979-8-89157-240-9 (digital)

Printed in the United States of America

DEDICATION

First and foremost, I want to dedicate not just this book of divine wisdom but my whole existence to the creator of such phenomenal creations as planet Earth, the sun, the moon, and humanity.

This powerful force is recognized by various cultures; therefore, the creator's name has variations.

The modern-day labels/names I will utilize to describe this energy source of supreme power is God or creator.

Also to my first and only child thus far, Mekhi King Ketter, You are loving, intelligent, strong, and extraordinary.

To my dear mother whom I witness overcome and endure trials and tribulations to provide the best for us when I was a child.

And to all loved ones, networks, and support systems with a focus on peace, purpose, and prosperity.

God bless <u>everyone.</u>

The best consolidation of affirmation quotes to inspire or
motivate humanity ever written in human history.

=The Messiah

THE INCEPTION

"To love yourself and others that are worthy
of such love is SELFLESS…
To live life only loving yourself is SELFISH."

=The Messiah

1

Taking the steps to improve yourself will improve your life.

=The Messiah

2

Building self-motivating values reduces dependence on external motivation (motivation from others). Receiving motivation from others is a good resource; however, building self-motivation (motivation from within) will give you, inner strength and radiance.

=The Messiah

3

Keep going until you obtain your goals through
physical determination and brainpower.

=The Messiah

4

If there are no present opportunities to progress,
formulate the opportunities yourself.

=The Messiah

5

You can always find ways to improve your life. There are different ways to improve yourself such as (1) brainpower improvements, (2) health improvements, (3) emotional stability improvements, (4) physical improvements, and (5) financial improvements.

=The Messiah

6

On the road to achieving success, you will encounter obstacles or hardships that will be misinterpreted as failures. However, you must overcome such obstacles or hardships to increase your chances of success.

=The Messiah

PERCEPTION

7

My powerful thoughts become powerful actions.

=The Messiah

8

Don't allow distractions to take you off
your chosen course of action.

=The Messiah

9

Make sure your foundation is strong; a strong
foundation prevents you from crumbling.

=The Messiah

10

When your awareness grows, what you expect from life increases.

=The Messiah

11

When you are doing positive, negative matters will
arise. Remain focused and firm on your path.

=The Messiah

12

Stay calm in the midst of chaos.

=The Messiah

13

Never become discouraged in displaying courage.

=The Messiah

14

Set your goals, then create and implement
a plan to reach your goals.

=The Messiah

15

Keep going, keep going! Stay on your path to obtain success.

=The Messiah

16

Focus on your vision, and it will unfold.

=The Messiah

17

If you stop focusing on your goals, visions of success will dissolve.

=The Messiah

18

If you don't believe you can achieve, then you will not receive.

=The Messiah

19

Keep building the best you.
The best results will come.

=The Messiah

20

Believing in yourself will enable others to believe in you.

=The Messiah

21

Being persistent and consistent leads to positive results.

=The Messiah

22

Don't allow others to set you back when you are moving forward

=The Messiah

23

Don't hate someone doing good.
Create ways to do good yourself.

=The Messiah

24

A display of honor is a reflection of honesty, loyalty, and respect.

=The Messiah

25

Turmoil creates distortion and misunderstanding.
Peace can lead to clarity and tranquility.

=The Messiah

26

Don't allow the negative behavior or lifestyle of
others to diminish your positive focus.

=The Messiah

27

Whether it's family or friends, never allow anyone to hold
you back from living a positive and peaceful life.

=The Messiah

28

Sincere family or friends that have your best interest
at heart will encourage positivity in your life and
discourage negativity that will destroy you.

=The Messiah

29

To trust the untrustworthy is a bond of dishonesty.

=The Messiah

30

Happiness is motivational and inspirational.
Never allow the unhappiness of others to diminish
your happiness or make you unhappy.

=The Messiah

31

A person that constantly displays characteristics
of hate possesses internal hatred.

=The Messiah

32

Never allow ignorance to penetrate your intelligence.

=The Messiah

33

If you doubt yourself others will doubt you. Have confidence in yourself, and others will have confidence in you.

=The Messiah

34

Don't hinder your positive internal or external
growth for the happiness of others.

=The Messiah

35

Inspiring others with happiness is good.
Being happy yourself is great.

=The Messiah

36

Don't go down a destructive path that reflects the desires of others
Stay on your constructive path that reflects your positive goals.

=The Messiah

37

If you compromise your peace for the chaotic lifestyle
of others, your life will become chaotic.

=The Messiah

38

Love yourself, even if you feel no love from others.

=The Messiah

39

If you are void of self-love, how can you fulfill others with love?

=The Messiah

40

Your radiant personality gives the environment radiance.

=The Messiah

41

Positive energy minimizes negative reactions.

=The Messiah

42

Letting go of negative energy is positive growth.

=The Messiah

43

Your truth creates a powerful aura that captivates others.

=The Messiah

44

Amazing you are! Amazing you will be!

=The Messiah

45

Your powerful focus empowers others.

=The Messiah

46

Your will to do good maintains goodness in you.

=The Messiah

47

The strength of your actions reflects the strength of your thoughts.

=The Messiah

48

You will encounter obstacles or hardships in your life. Allow
such encounters to make you stronger, not weaker.

=The Messiah

49

Never allow a culture of hate to make you become hateful.

=The Messiah

50

Seeking truth dissolves untruth.

=The Messiah

51

Fortitude is a key component when one
encounters adversities or adversaries.

=The Messiah

52

Going down the right path is never wrong.

=The Messiah

53

Distant yourself from ignorance that complicates your life.

=The Messiah

54

Strive for advancement, and always enhance your abilities to do so.

=The Messiah

55

You can live right despite the wrongs committed
against you by obtaining prosperity.

=The Messiah

56

The strength of one can put strength in many.

=The Messiah

57

Studying the world is good for external knowledge.
Studying yourself is great and reflects knowledge
of self, which is internal knowledge.

=The Messiah

58

Cause CONSTRUCTION in your life, not DESTRUCTION.

=The Messiah

59

Never allow the doubt of others to create doubt in you.

=The Messiah

60

Your thoughts come to life when you take some form of action.

=The Messiah

61

Learn to adapt and you will become adaptable.

=The Messiah

62

What you build extends from a concept, which
is derived from the thought process.

=The Messiah

63

Look ahead.

Be ahead.

=The Messiah

64

Your values establish your boundaries.

=The Messiah

65

Good health is VITAL. Wealth is a great resource.

=The Messiah

66

Having inner peace is essential to remain peaceful with others.

=The Messiah

67

Build your will to live.

Build your will to survive.

There are several ways to increase your chances of

obtaining your goals and above are great ways.

=The Messiah

68

Being happy with yourself builds self-confidence, which dissolves self-doubt.

=The Messiah

69

If you seek true loyalty, honesty, and trust, that's rare
but valuable qualities; you must exude those same
qualities to whomever you seek such qualities from.

=The Messiah

70

Cultivate the gift or gifts within you that others don't recognize but you realize.

=The Messiah

71

Always find time to focus on your health; the investment is worth it.

=The Messiah

72

Brain health is important to combat stress and depression
or to dissolve unwanted thoughts that can trigger such.

=The Messiah

73

Human activity or activity in general, environments,
and matters that relax your brain create an
internal feeling of serenity and tranquility.

=The Messiah

74

Take care of your health early in your life,
and it will benefit you in later years.

=The Messiah

75

In between times of taking care of others,
find time to take care of your health.

=The Messiah

76

Healthy thoughts lead to healthy living…
unhealthy thoughts lead to unhealthy living.

=The Messiah

77

Push yourself past your own expectations.

=The Messiah

78

To obtain happiness, you must have the inner strength to let go of matters that create unhappiness in your life.

=The Messiah

79

Self-control allows one to remain in control of their emotions.

=The Messiah

80

Always maintain the determination to take care of your family
and yourself, and opportunities will present themselves.

=The Messiah

81

When you doubt yourself, your actions
reflect constant procrastination.

=The Messiah

82

When you are on a journey to improve your life,
hardships, obstacles, or pitfalls will occur.
Success is attained by those who navigate around such disturbances.

=The Messiah

83

Focus prevents failure.

=The Messiah

84

If your faith brings you peace, happiness, and spiritual elevation, others around you will feel your positive energy.

=The Messiah

85

Communication is a key component to the progression of relations.

=The Messiah

86

Planning ahead with different viewpoints displays foresight.
Having the ability to learn from events after
it has occurred displays HINDSIGHT.

=The Messiah

87

Studying yourself will improve your overall studies.

=The Messiah

88

If you never give up on your path to excel,
you will become excellent.

=The Messiah

89

Life is precious to those who cultivate their lives.

=The Messiah

90

To live a life empty of vision, such life will
be empty of progress or prosperity.

=The Messiah

91

Take the initiative to improve your health, no
matter your age group or health conditions.

=The Messiah

92

Doing good is just as important as feeling good.

=The Messiah

93

Success comes to those who work hard for themselves or others.

=The Messiah

94

If you DISTINGUISH yourself from others…others
cannot EXTINGUISH your uniqueness.

=The Messiah

95

Never allow temptations to tempt you off the path of your choice.

=The Messiah

96

Believe in yourself as you will believe in your
chosen religion or belief system.

=The Messiah

97

Positive thoughts and positive action lead to a
positive path enriched with a positive network.

=The Messiah

98

Knowledge is the collection of information or data obtained to raise one awareness. Wisdom is having the insight and understanding to decode the knowledge you attained and learning how to apply learned knowledge, which elevates your awareness. This reflects knowledge, wisdom, and understanding.

=The Messiah

99

If you learn and understand yourself, it's easier
to learn and understand others.

=The Messiah

100

If you keep rising, that will prevent you from falling.

=The Messiah

101

Remember you can be well, do well, or get well;
the key is to dissolve your self-doubt, take the
initiative, and maintain determination.

=The Messiah

About the Author

Born and raised in a God-fearing household located in Brooklyn, New York, prepared Michael for the ungodly activity that plagued many African American communities in the 1980s, 1990s, and 2000s. This was the beginning of intense studying and training to awaken the gifts within Michael, as a being that can decode, complex coded messages and visions, combined with much more. Overcoming the perils that led many in the African American community to early death or imprisonment inspired Michael to do more.

Becoming a carpenter was Michael's first great vision as a child, and as an adult years ago, he fulfilled that vision by completing two years of school to become a certified carpenter. However, Michael's vision to do more didn't end after his successful completion of carpentry. Wanting to do more for communities impacted by injustice sent Michael back to school and training to become a counselor and advocate. Understanding such credentials opens the door to assist many Michael was guided toward the creation of his first mission (Strong America's Recovery Mission).

And now the messages and visions, which have been an internal compass within Michael since his youth, are guiding him into his next phase: a book writer/author.